Homebirth Baby

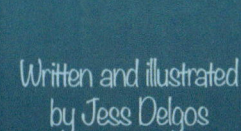

Written and illustrated
by Jess Delgos

I was not born in a hospital,
Or on the road along the way.
My parents chose to be at home,
When it became my birthing day.

My parents were not lazy,
Or even unprepared.
They did lots of research,
And made a birthing plan with care.

For the birth my parents dreamed,
They listened to mind and heart.
And chose the place and people,
To nurture my journey's start.

So my parents made a birthing room,
Inside our warm and cosy home.
The room was quiet and dark,
So I felt safe entering the unknown.

We had a magical midwife,
Who could hear me from outside.
She could even amplify my heartbeat,
Sparking joyful and reassured cries.

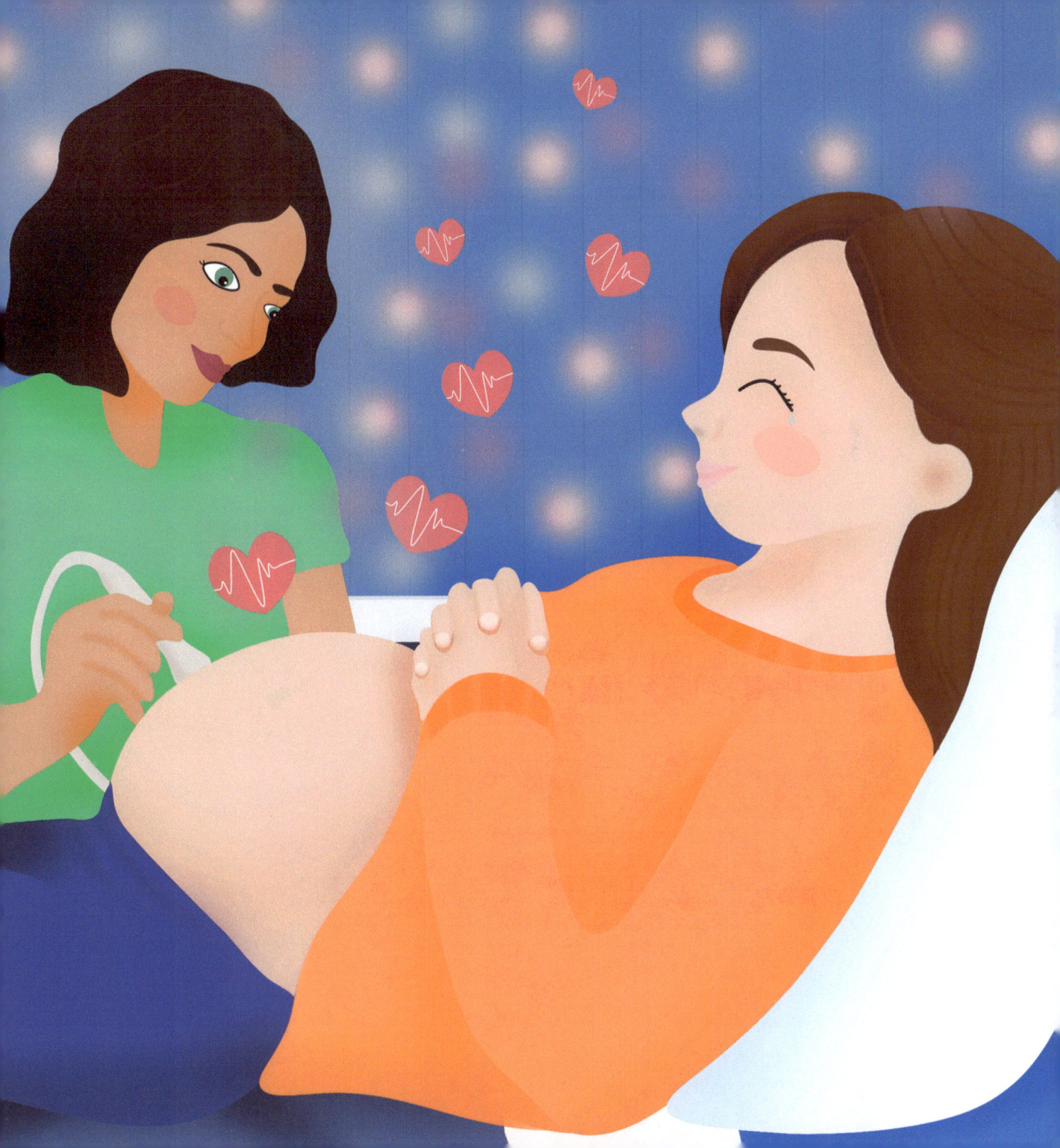

She cared for our little family,
Always checking that I was okay.
She supported my parents,
To birth me their chosen way.

My mother's body is wise,
And knew just what to do.
It prepared the birth canal,
So I could dance the whole way through.

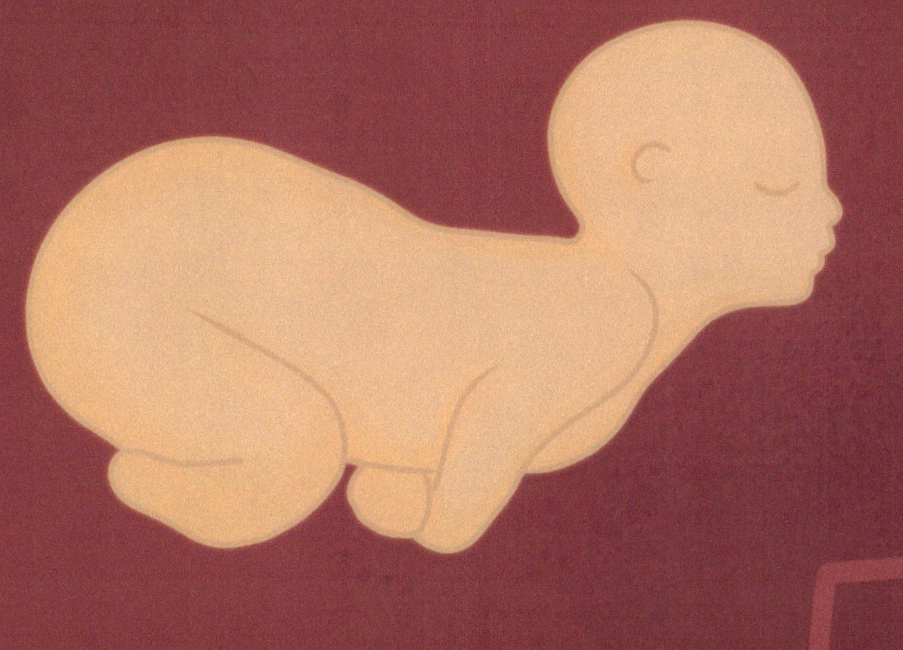

Some babies dance slower than others,
Thank you mum for trusting the process.
For knowing I'll arrive when I'm ready,
For your patience and your focus.

I was birthed into a pool,
When surfaced I took my first breath.
Instantly you gave me the comfort I needed,
Snuggled into your warm motherly chest.

I gripped on to one of dad's big fingers,
Still tethered by our cord.
In my parents embrace,
Was where I felt most adored.

Hungry after my long journey,
I chest crawled up to latch.
Suckling for milk and comfort,
Constantly cradled and free to nap.

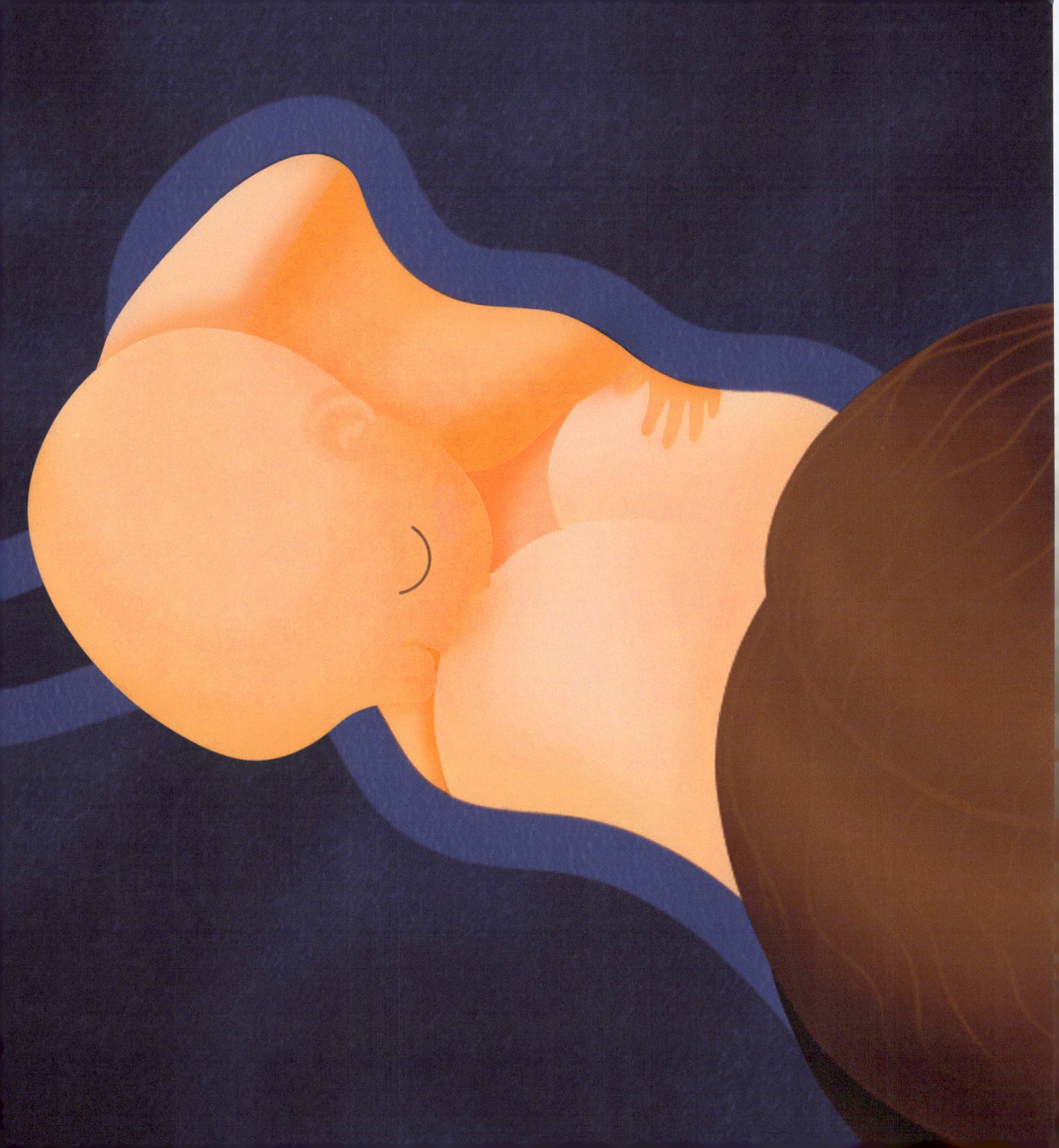

For days we stayed in our love bubble,
Just my family and me.
The magical Midwife visited from time to time,
To check my weight and wees.

My parents reflect on my birth,
And tell me it was perfect.
They say doing things a little different,
Is so incredibly worth it!

My birth

The story of my birth

www.ingramcontent.com/pod-product-compliance
Lightning Source LLC
Chambersburg PA
CBHW041407160426
42811CB00103B/1546